A FIRST LOOK BOOK

The Planets

Michael Jay

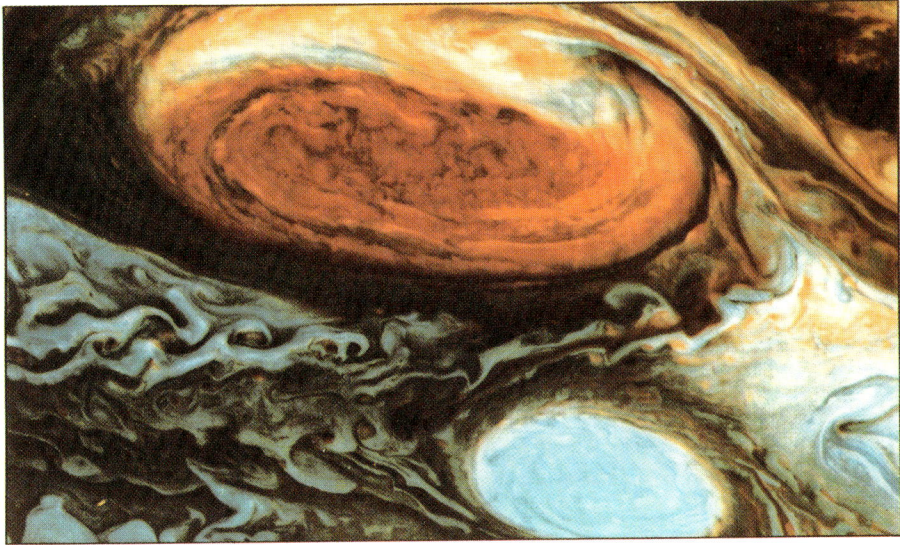

Franklin Watts

London   New York   Sydney   Toronto

The cover shows the nine
planets to scale.

The previous page shows a
picture of Jupiter's Red Spot.
This is thought to be a vast,
hurricane-like storm in the
atmosphere of the giant planet.
The storm has raged for
hundreds of years. The red spot
is big enough to swallow the
Earth several times over.

© 1987 Franklin Watts
First published in Great Britain
1987 by
Franklin Watts
12a Golden Square
London W1

First published in the USA by
Franklin Watts Inc.
387 Park Avenue South
New York
N.Y. 10016

UK ISBN 0 86313 495 5
US ISBN 0-531-10278-5
Library of Congress Catalog
Card Number: 86-50636

Designed by
David Jefferis/Sunrise Books

Illustrated by
Drawing Attention
Robert Burns
Hayward Art Group
Michael Roffe

Photographs supplied by
NASA

Technical consultant
Mat Irvine FBIS

Printed in Great Britain by
Cambus Litho, East Kilbride

A FIRST LOOK BOOK

The Planets

Contents

The Solar System	4
At the dawn of time	6
Heavenly wanderers	8
Mercury	10
Venus, superhot world	12
Blue planet Earth	14
Mars, the red planet	16
Mighty Jupiter	18
Saturn, the ringworld	20
Uranus	22
Neptune and Pluto	24
Moons big and small	26
More worlds in space?	28
Spaceprobes	30
Glossary	32
Index	

The Solar System

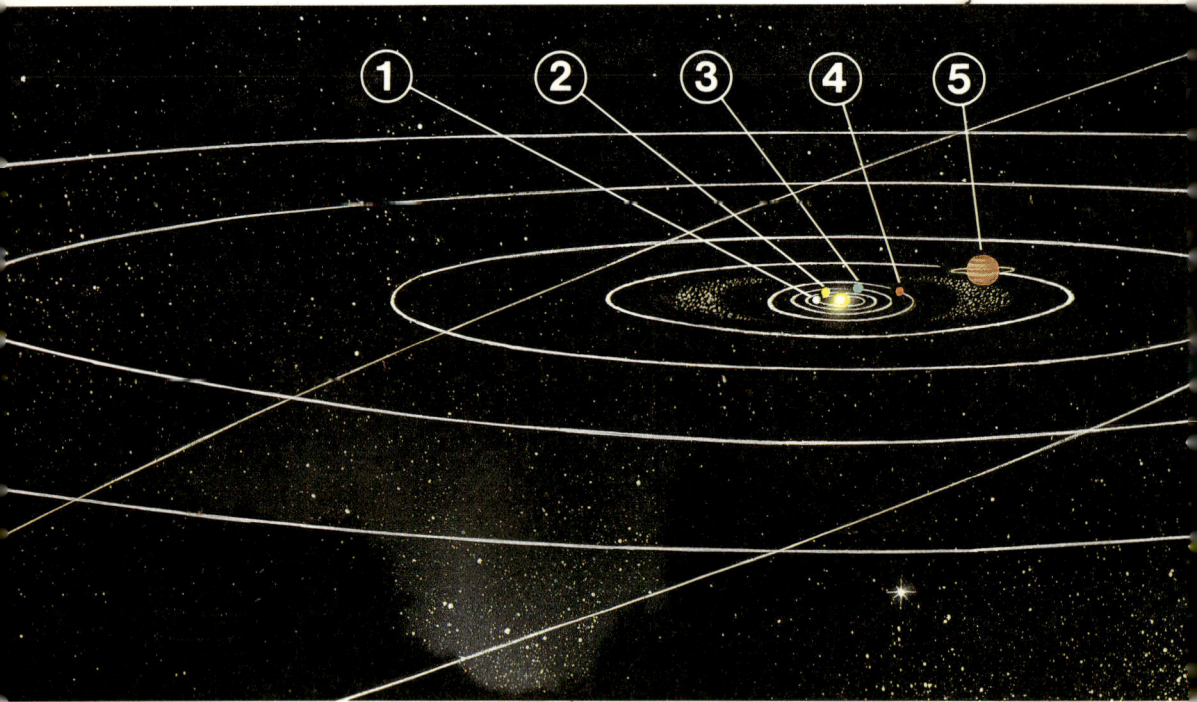

The Solar System is the name given to the planets, moons and other cosmic material which whirl through space around the Sun.

Our knowledge of the Solar System has increased enormously since spacecraft have been sent on exploring missions far into space. Only Neptune and Pluto have not been closely inspected by visiting spaceprobes.

△ Shown above are the planets. Each moves in a nearly circular path around the Sun. This is its orbit. **1** Mercury. **2** Venus. **3** Earth. **4** Mars. **5** Jupiter. **6** Saturn. **7** Uranus. **8** Neptune. **9** Pluto.

▷ The chart shows some planetary statistics.

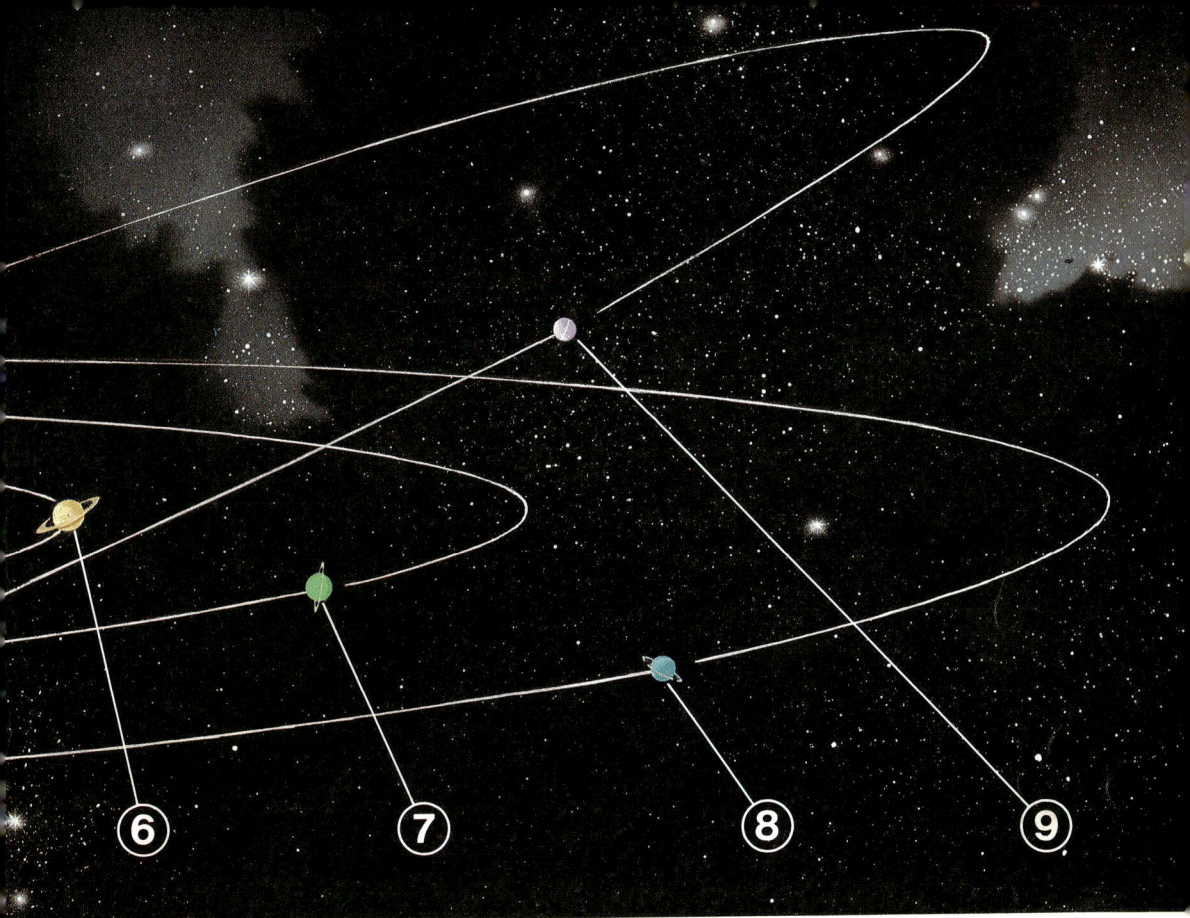

Planet	Diameter	Day (time taken to spin on axis)	Year (time taken to orbit the Sun)
1 Mercury	4,878 km (3,031 miles)	59 Earth days	88 Earth days
2 Venus	12,104 km (7,521 miles)	243 days	225 days
3 Earth	12,756 km (7,926 miles)	23 hr 56 min	365.25 days
4 Mars	6,794 km (4,221 miles)	24 hr 37.5 min	687 days
5 Jupiter	142,800 km (88,735 miles)	9 hr 50.5 min	11.8 years
6 Saturn	120,000 km (74,568 miles)	10 hr 40 min	29.5 years
7 Uranus	51,800 km (32,188 miles)	16 hr 48 min	84 years
8 Neptune	49,500 km (30,759 miles)	18 hr	164.8 years
9 Pluto	2,400 km (1,491 miles)	6 days 9 hr	248 years

At the dawn of time

△ When the Solar System formed, the universe was already 10,000 million years old. Scientists think it exploded into existence as a "Big Bang" of energy and matter.

Scientists think that the Solar System formed about 5,000 million years ago.

At first there was nothing but a cloud of gas and dust between the stars. Gradually, over millions of years, the gas and dust collected to form clumps of material.

At the centre of the swirling cloud, the gas began to heat up and glow. The Sun was born, flooding the early Solar System with light and energy.

There was still much cosmic debris in space, swept up by the growing masses of the still-forming planets. The crater-scarred surfaces of most of the planets show the mighty impacts of the early space bombardment.

There is still plenty of space rubble left over from the birth of the Solar System. Thousands of rocks drift between Mars and Jupiter. They are known as the asteroids. Further out, uncounted millions of comets exist.

◁ The main picture shows the early Solar System. Vast clouds of gas and dust collect to form the Sun, planets and moons.

△ This picture shows the Pleiades, a group of young stars, forming from gas and dust. There may be planets forming too.

Heavenly wanderers

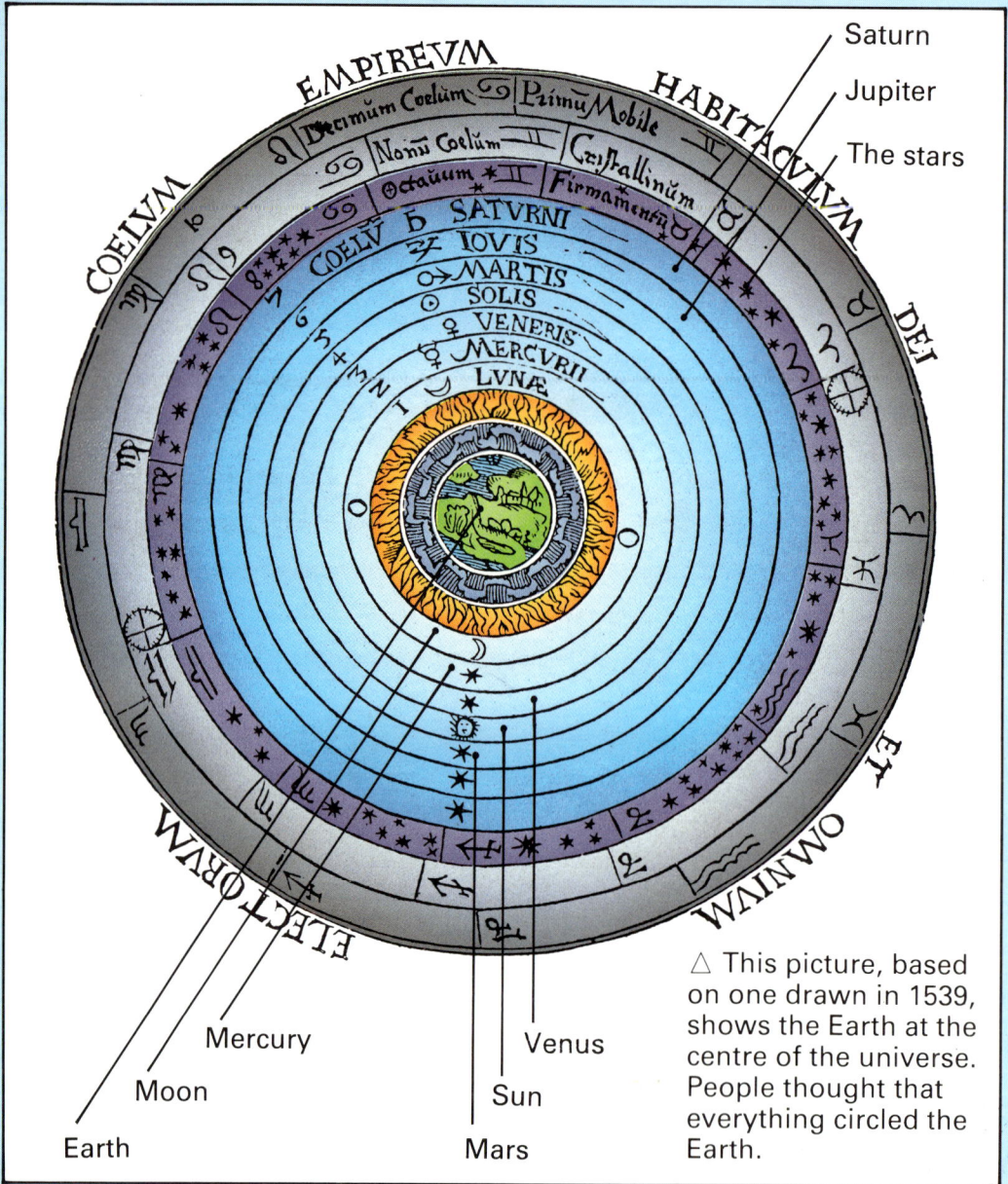

Saturn

Jupiter

The stars

EMPIREVM

HABITACVLVM

COELVM

Decimũm Coelũm

Primũ Mobile

Nōnũ Coelũm

Octauũ

Cristallinũm

Firmamentũ

COELV ♄ SATVRNI

♃ IOVIS

♂ MARTIS

☉ SOLIS

♀ VENERIS

☿ MERCVRII

LVNÆ

DEI

ELECTORVM

OMNIVM ET

Earth

Moon

Mercury

Sun

Mars

Venus

△ This picture, based on one drawn in 1539, shows the Earth at the centre of the universe. People thought that everything circled the Earth.

Our knowledge of the planets is fairly recent – Pluto, the furthest planet from the Sun, was not discovered until 1930. And there are astronomers who think there may be a mystery Planet "X" out there, still awaiting discovery.

Peoples of ancient civilizations who observed the skies were intrigued by those "stars" which appeared to move slowly across the heavens. In fact, these were the five planets most easily visible – Mercury, Venus, Mars, Jupiter and Saturn.

The ancient Greeks named them as wanderers or "planetas", the word we still use today. To these people, it seemed obvious that the Earth was the middle of things. Moon, planets, Sun and stars were thought to be fixed in crystal spheres, rotating about the Earth.

In the 16th century, a Polish clergyman, Nicolaus Copernicus, suggested that the planets went around the Sun. But it was not until 1621 that a German astronomer, Johannes Kepler, worked out laws to explain the motions of the planets accurately.

△ Pluto was found by Clyde Tombaugh in 1930. He studied photographs of the night sky and one "star" appeared to move. It was in just the right place to be another planet, the ninth world, Pluto. The pictures above show what Tombaugh was looking for – a speck of light jumping across the star field.

Mercury

Mercury is a world of fierce heat and savage cold. By day, the Sun burns Mercury to a noon temperature of 410°C. At night, temperatures drop to a shivering minus 170°C. By contrast, the hottest temperature ever recorded on Earth is just 58°C, the coldest minus 88.3°C.

The hot days of Mercury are explained by its nearness to the Sun, just 58 million km (36 million miles) away. At night, the heat simply leaks into space. Mercury has no air, which would act as a blanket to keep in much of the heat.

Most of our knowledge of Mercury comes from the Mariner 10 spaceprobe which flew by the planet in 1974 and 1975. It showed that the surface is covered with thousands of craters.

The biggest crater photographed by Mariner 10 was the Caloris Basin. It is 1,300 km (808 miles) across.

△ Morning on Mercury. The Sun bakes the landscape at temperatures hot enough to melt lead.

◁ Mariner 10 flies by the blasted, crater-covered face of Mercury. Cameras aboard the craft gave scientists their first close-up look at the planet nearest the Sun.

11

△ A Russian Venera probe surveys the superheated rocks on the surface of Venus. Spacecraft don't last long here. The heat and pressure soon wreck the toughest machine.

▷ To human eyes, the clouds of Venus shine a featureless white. But special filters reveal complex cloud patterns like these.

12

Venus, superhot world

Venus appears in the sky as a beautiful morning or evening star. The Romans named the planet after their goddess of love and beauty. The reality is very different – Venus has a choking atmosphere and roasts at temperatures hotter than Mercury. At ground level, the temperature soars to 470°C.

This is because Venus has been over-whelmed by the "greenhouse effect". Like the panes of glass in a greenhouse, the atmosphere of Venus lets heat in and traps it, so the planet never cools off at night.

The atmosphere is mainly carbon dioxide gas. There is so much of it that the atmosphere crushes the surface with a pressure 90 times than on Earth. Spaceprobes have survived for only short periods before failing under the heat and pressure.

The only way Venus resembles the Earth is in size – it is just a little smaller.

△ Radar penetrates the dense clouds of Venus as if they were invisible. This radar picture shows highland regions of Venus, computer coded to show up bright yellow.

Blue planet Earth

△ The blue planet, Earth. Our world is misnamed really – over 70 per cent of the surface is covered with water!

Spaceprobes have shown that our own world is unique in the Solar System. It seems to be the only planet with life.

Before space travel, many scientists hoped that Venus might be a steamy jungle world. Others thought that Mars might have some plant life.

The Earth circles the Sun in a fairly narrow band, known as the ecosphere. If the Earth goes too near the Sun its life-giving water boils away. Too far

away and the water freezes to ice. Only on our world are there oceans of liquid water, without which, life would not have developed.

The Earth is tilted too. The poles alternately face towards, and away from, the Sun. This gives us the seasons and ensures that only a few places on the planet remain frozen for long or are permanently "boiled" by the Sun's rays.

△ Crashing waves break over a rocky coastline. Earth is the only planet where water can be found in all its three states – as a gas, as a liquid, or frozen as ice.

Mars, the red planet

▽ Robot surveyor-wheels like these could be rolling on the deserts of the red planet by the late 1990s, if current plans get the go-ahead. Here, surveyors are shown inspecting the bottom of Valles Marineris.

Mars is a world of shifting sands and rusty-red deserts. When two Viking spaceprobes landed there in 1976, their chief job was to search for life. The robot explorers had small laboratories and scoop arms to test the soil for living things. None were found. Mars

seems too dry and cold.

Other Martian discoveries were more exciting. Olympus Mons rises 26 km (16 miles) above the desert. It is a volcano 600 km (370 miles) across. The huge valley of Valles Marineris is four times deeper and ten times longer than Earth's Grand Canyon.

Many of the Martian channels look as if they were carved out by rivers. Water now frozen as ice at the poles may once have flowed on the surface.

▽ A computer-coloured picture of Olympus Mons, taken by NASA's Viking Orbiter. Olympus Mons is (so far as we know) the biggest volcano in the Solar System.

Mighty Jupiter

Jupiter is the biggest planet of all. It has 16 known moons, several of which are as big as small planets.

Jupiter has no proper surface – it is made mostly of hydrogen gas. The atmosphere of Jupiter moves in swirling cloud belt patterns. Nothing is permanent, though one feature, the Great Red Spot, has been seen by astronomers for over 300 years.

Below the cloud tops, the atmosphere is thousands of kilometres deep. There is no way to look at the bottom layers, but scientists think that the weight of the gases eventually squashes the hydrogen so much that it behaves like a liquid metal. There may be a metallic "ocean" forever hidden from our view.

Jupiter has a faint dust ring. This could be the remains of a moon that drifted too close and got ripped apart by the gravity of the huge planet.

△ A future spaceprobe parachutes through the upper layers of Jupiter's atmosphere. Eventually the craft will be crushed by the enormous pressures further down.

▷ Astronauts standing on Callisto, moon of Jupiter, would get this spectacular view of Jupiter rising above the horizon. Near the ultra-thin ring you can make out the small globes of other moons.

Saturn, the ringworld

△ Above, Voyager 2 cruises past the beautiful rings of Saturn, backlit by the rays of the distant Sun.

Saturn has the biggest and best ring system. It also has the most moons, 23 in all, including the biggest moon in the Solar System, Titan.

The rings are divided into thousands of individual ringlets. They look like

the grooves in an LP record, and are made of countless billions of chunks of water ice.

One ring, the F ring, seems to defy the laws of physics. It is twisted and braided, with strands that cross and recross like lengths of wool. Two small "Shepherd" moons, called S26 and S27, are thought to keep the F ring in place. Their gravity pull is probably responsible for the twisting as well.

△ Close-up pictures taken by Voyager reveal the complex and strange nature of the rings.

Uranus

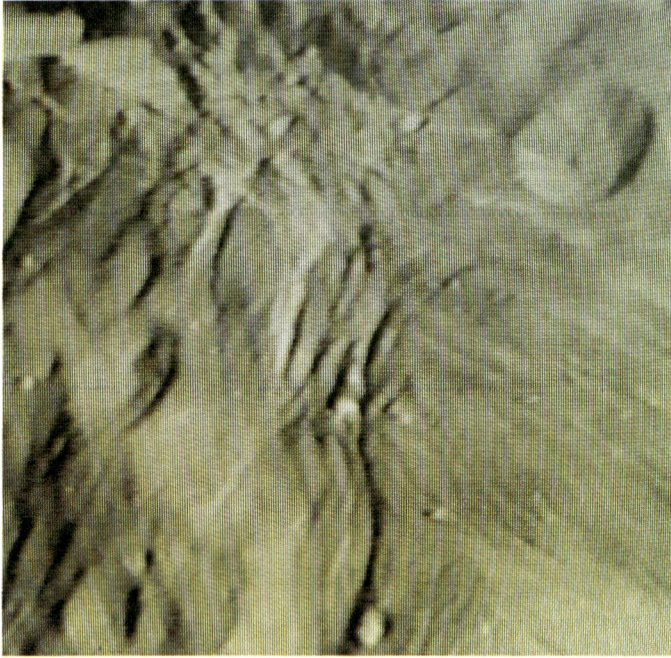

△ Miranda, moon of Uranus. This picture was taken by Voyager 2. The moon has craters, cracks, ridges and canyons. Miranda is one of 16 moons orbiting Uranus.

Uranus is another ringworld. Its rings are dark and thin. Voyager 2 flew by Uranus in 1986 and detected 10 rings, but scientists think that as many as 100 fainter ones may exist.

Unlike any other planet, Uranus spins on its side, with its poles facing towards and away from the Sun. One theory suggests that Uranus might have collided with an Earth-sized planet. The force of the collision may

have destroyed the small planet and knocked Uranus sideways.

The atmosphere of Uranus is mainly methane gas, which gives the planet a bluish-green appearance. The atmosphere is quite clear, with some haze and a few clouds.

One mystery discovered by Voyager 2 was that the sunlit pole of Uranus seems slightly cooler than the pole facing away from the Sun!

△ From Miranda, Uranus could look like this – a giant, blue-green globe, rising above frozen wastes of rock and rubble.

Neptune and Pluto

△ Voyager 2 may get a view like this in 1989. Here, the moon Triton passes in front of the distant Sun.

Below, the diagram shows Neptune's curious "arc" rings. Instead of complete rings, they seem to be segments of a circle.

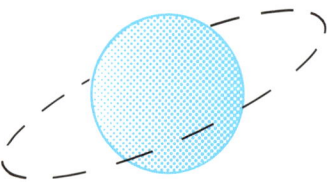

Neptune and Pluto are the furthest planets from the Sun. Their orbits cross, so that from 1979 until 1999, Pluto passes inside the orbit of Neptune. So, at present, Neptune is the outermost world. But there is no danger of the two planets colliding, as their orbits are at different angles.

Neptune seems similar to Uranus in many ways. It is a little larger, but shares a similar blue-green colour. It

has a curious ring system though – the rings seem to be divided into segments instead of being complete. Voyager 2 should clear up this, and other mysteries, when it passes Neptune in 1989.

Pluto is the smallest planet, just half the size of Mercury. It has a moon called Charon which was discovered in 1978. Like the other outer planets, Pluto is icy-cold. Temperatures are hundreds of degrees below zero.

△ Morning on Pluto. Compare this chilly scene with that of Mercury shown on page 11. Shining over a lake of frozen methane, the Sun's rays boil off cold wisps of methane gas.

Hanging above this frigid scene is Charon, the single moon of Pluto.

Moons big and small

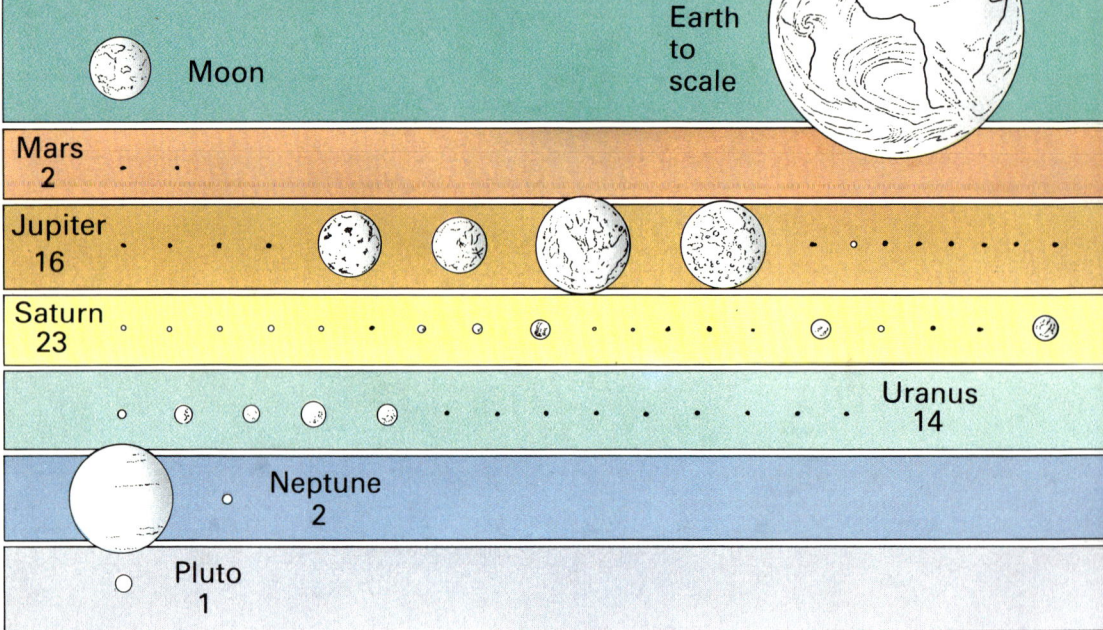

Moon

Earth to scale

Mars
2

Jupiter
16

Saturn
23

Uranus
14

Neptune
2

Pluto
1

△ Here are the 59 known moons of the Solar System, shown to scale. It is likely that Neptune has several more moons awaiting discovery.

All the planets except Mercury and Venus have moons. Look up in the night sky and you can see Earth's own Moon, just "next door" as space distances go. The moon is covered with craters. These are the scars of meteorite strikes. Millions of years ago, countless chunks of space rock slammed into the Moon. Some of them punched through the Moon's outer crust. Hot lava bubbled up from inside and spread

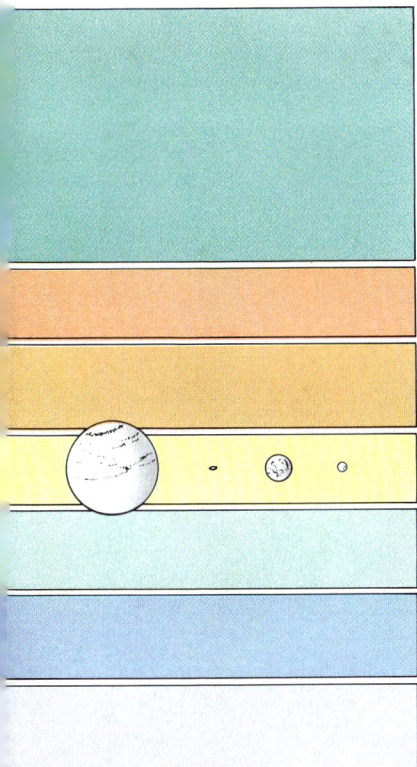

across the surface to form the "seas" and "oceans" of the Moon.

Moons of other worlds range from tiny Phobos and Deimos orbiting Mars, to huge Titan. The moons of Mars are just a few kilometres across, with so little gravity that if you jumped up on one, you wouldn't come down again! Titan has a smoggy orange atmosphere, mainly of nitrogen gas.

△ This view shows the sulphur volcanoes of Io, moon of Jupiter. Mighty explosions throw plumes of gas hundreds of kilometres above the surface.

More worlds in space?

△ If Planet Ten exists, it will be a frozen world, lost in the outer reaches of the Solar System. From there, the Sun would appear as no more than a bright star, providing little light or heat.

After he discovered Pluto in 1930, Clyde Tombaugh carried on planet-hunting. He didn't find any other worlds, but astronomers think that a tenth planet could exist.

Small changes in the orbital movements of Uranus and Neptune show that there may be something in deep space beyond Pluto. Various ideas for the "something" include another planet or a dark star. But, at

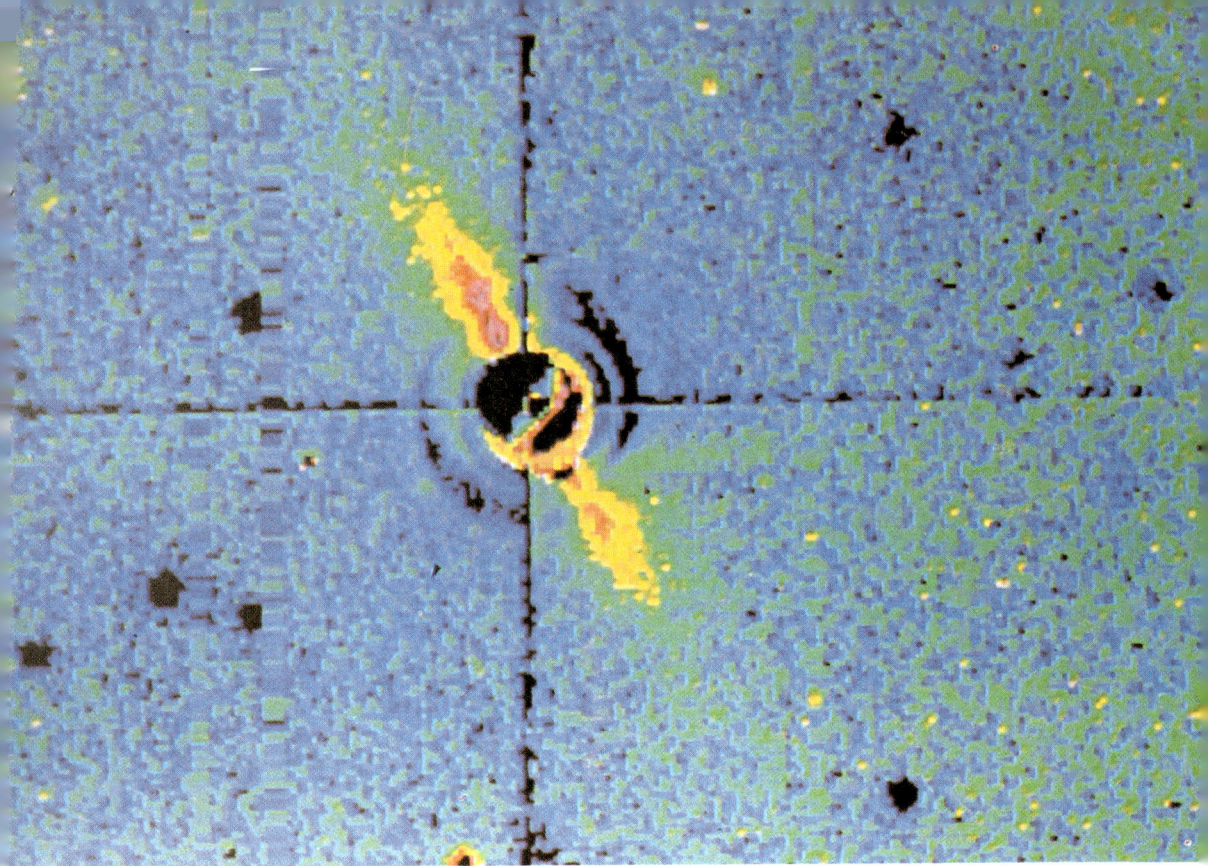

present, there are no more clues. So Planet Ten remains a mystery.

Looking further away, astronomers are searching for planets of other stars. This is a difficult job, as the distances are so vast. But the picture above shows what seems to be another system of planets forming from gas and dust, just the way we think the Solar System came into being, nearly 5,000 million years ago.

△ This is the first view of planets forming around another star. The star is Beta Pictoris and the "wings" either side are our edge-on view of a disc of gas and dust. The material is almost certainly collecting to form planets. Another star, called VB8, has a companion which is midway between the size of a star and a planet.

29

Spaceprobes

Spacecraft like these have landed on or flown by most of the planets.

Russian space probes have studied Venus and Halley's comet.

Mariner 10 probed Venus and took over 5,000 pictures of Mercury.

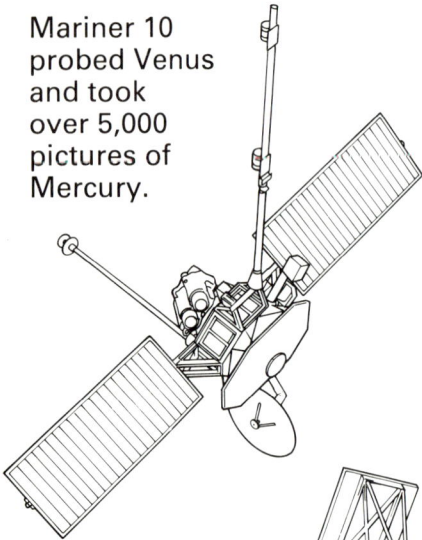

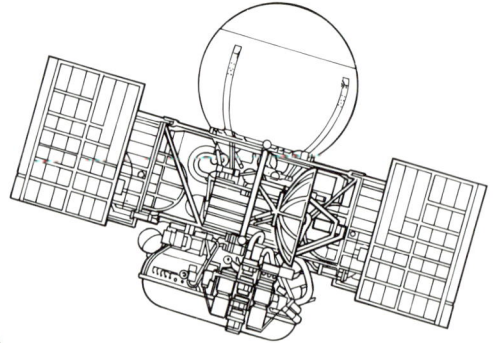

Voyagers have probed Jupiter, Saturn and Uranus

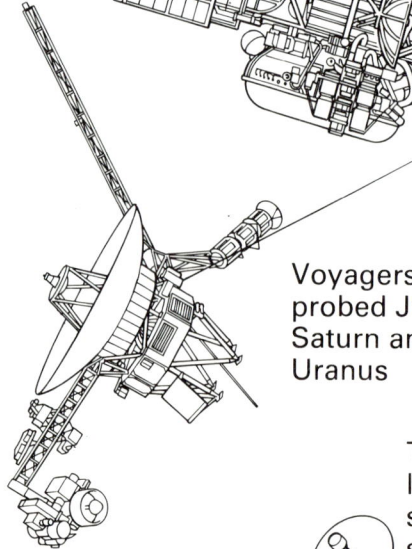

Two Viking landers sampled the soil of Mars.

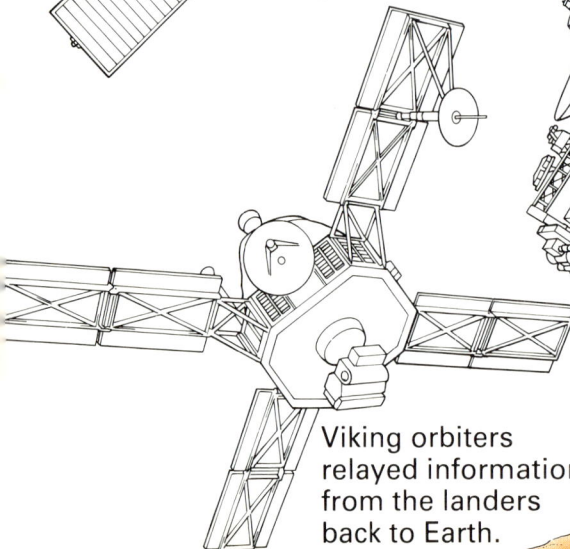

Viking orbiters relayed information from the landers back to Earth.

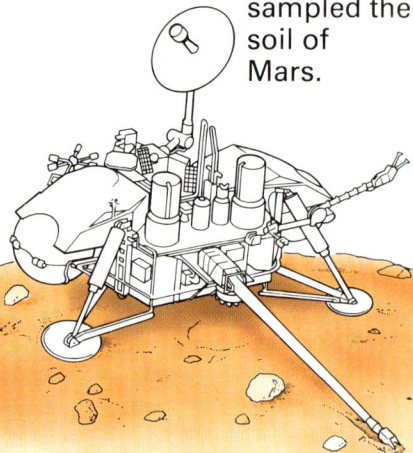

Glossary

Here are some explanations for the technical words used in this book.

Asteroid
One of the "minor planets". There are thousands of them in a belt mostly between Mars and Jupiter. The biggest, Ceres, is about 1000 km (620 miles) across.
   The biggest asteroids are round, like planets. Small ones come in all shapes. There is even one shaped like a peanut!

Big Bang
Theory which says the Universe began as an explosion of energy.

Brown dwarf
Space object which is halfway between the size of a star and a planet. The star VB8 has such a dwarf companion. It is an object about 10 times as massive as Jupiter. It has a surface temperature of 1,000°C.

Charon
Only moon of Pluto. It is about half the size of Pluto.

Comet
Space object made of ice and dust which occasionally approaches the Sun. A long tail can develop when the Sun's rays are strong enough to vaporize the ice of the comet nucleus.

Day
The length of time it takes a planet to rotate once about its axis. The Earth's day is just short of 24 hours.

Gravity
Force of attraction between objects. Large objects have a strong gravity pull. Less massive ones have weaker gravity.

Greenhouse effect
Where a thick atmosphere traps heat, like the windows of a greenhouse.

Meteorite
Chunk of space rock which hits a planet. Meteorite speeds can be very fast – often over 80 km/sec (50 miles/sec).

Orbit
The curving path one space object takes around another.
   Most planet orbits are almost circular. That of Pluto is more of an oval, so sometimes the planet passes inside the orbit of Neptune.

Year
The length of time it takes a planet to complete one orbit around the Sun. The Earth takes 365 days. Distant Pluto takes 248 Earth years to complete its orbit.

Index

asteroids 6, 31
astronauts 18
astronomers 9, 28
atmosphere 13, 18, 23, 27

Beta Pictoris 29
"Big Bang" 29
Brown Dwarf 31

Callisto 18
Caloris Basin 10
carbon dioxide 13
Ceres 31
Charon 25, 31
comets 6, 31
Copernicus 9
crater 6, 10, 22, 26

day 5, 31
diameter 5
Diemos 27

Earth 4, 5, 8, 9, 13, 14, 15, 26
ecosphere 14

F ring 21

Grand Canyon 17
gravity 31
Great Red Spot 18
greenhouse effect 31

Halley's comet 30

hydrogen 18

Io 27

Jupiter 4, 5, 6, 8, 9, 18, 27, 30, 31

Kepler 9

laboratories 16
lava 26

Mariner 10, 10, 11, 30
Mars 4, 5, 6, 8, 9, 14, 16, 17, 27, 30, 31
Mercury 4, 5, 8, 9, 10, 11, 13, 26, 30
meteorite 31
Miranda 22, 23
Moon 8, 9, 26
moons 4, 7, 18, 20, 26, 27

NASA 17
Neptune 4, 5, 24, 25, 26, 28

Olympus Mons 17
orbit 31

Phobos 27
planetas 9
Pleiades 7
Pluto 4, 5, 9, 24, 25, 28, 31

poles 15, 17, 22, 23
pressure 13

radar 13
robots 16, 17
Romans 13

Saturn 4, 5, 8, 9, 20, 30
shepherd moons 21
Solar System 4, 6, 7, 14, 17, 20, 26, 28
spaceprobes 4, 10, 13, 14, 30
stars 7
Sun 4, 6, 7, 9, 10, 11, 14, 15, 22, 24, 28, 31

temperature 10, 13, 25, 31
Titan 20, 27
Tombaugh 9, 28

Uranus 4, 5, 22, 24, 28, 30

Valles Marineras 16, 17
VB8, 29, 31
Venera 12
Venus 4, 5, 8, 9, 12, 13, 14, 26, 30
Viking spaceprobe 16, 30
volcano 17, 27
voyager 2, 20, 21, 22, 24, 25, 30